undertow

undertow

poems

anne shaw

A Karen & Michael Braziller Book
Persea Books / NEW YORK

Persea Books, Inc.
853 Broadway
New York, NY 10003

Library of Congress Cataloging-in-Publication Data
Shaw, Anne.
Undertow : poems / Anne Shaw.
p. cm.
"A Karen & Michael Braziller book."
ISBN 978-0-89255-338-9 (trade pbk. : alk. paper)
I. Title.
PS3619.H3916U53 2007
811'.6--dc22

2007025143

Designed by Dinah Fried

First Edition
Printed in the United States of America

for alane

acknowledgements

Grateful acknowledgement is made to the following publications, in which these poems first appeared, sometimes in slightly different forms.

Crania:	"The Cipher," "Having Been Put to Bed"
The Cresset	"Crossing to Chebeague: December in Casco Bay"
Gulf Coast	"Hymn"
Hayden's Ferry Review	"In Medias Res"
Natural Bridge	"The Visions at Lascaux"
New American Writing	"Aegean," "Shibboleth"
Phoebe	"Enumeration," "Lineage"
Wisconsin Poets' Calendar	"Formulary for a Winter Landscape"

Deepest gratitude to my mentors, Eric Pankey and Carolyn Forché, and to my teachers and colleagues at George Mason University, without whom this book would not exist. I am also indebted to numeous readers whose careful attention helped shape these pages: Andrew Feld, Mary Crow, Stacy Szymaszek Dianne Timblin, Jean Preston, and Alan Wallace, as well as the particpants of the first Colrain Poetry Manuscript Conference. Special thanks to all the folks at Persea, and especially to Gabe Fried, for his patient guidance, insight, and support.

For sharing their homes and stories, my gratitude to the people of Khao Lak, Thailand, and Communidad Amazanga, Ecuador: you touched me deeply.

Finally, their support and belief over the course of many years, warm thanks to John Shaw, Linda Kramer, Anne Kingsbury, Karl Gartung, and Richard Roe. To Alane, for the dark hours: love beyond words.

contents

3

4

I

caution, freight

In the river of my dream I'm ankle-deep
in the water's muddy froth, my cuffs rolled up. A manatee or alligator

swims at me and rises, hugely brown. It's the size of a submarine
with dull, enormous eyes. You call it *hell dog* and begin

to flee. The narrator of the dream informs: *The hell dog rises from the river,*
fixes its eyes on the head of its target prey. I'm about

to miss my flight for Panama, having dallied too long in your arms.
Meanwhile, on the coffee table, an orange deer circles its glass.

It is a small restitution. Apricot syrup and hearts of palm
stiffen with dust in the pantry. These things keep.

How each mahogany chair leg prefigures elegy. Of memory,
permit a skep. Of pollen, suffice it to say, a single grain.

Later, we walk through winter, each small hesitation recorded in the snow.
Narrow the spans: remorse, intent. Narrow the bands of light.

We do not indulge in jungles, savannahs, or the sky.
The seconds tick by like boxcars. One mississippi. Two mississippi. Three.

hymn

The pink troll of our decade snickers from under its bridge
as the country goes crazy for jesus and the grey men
in the alley start to stink. I am humming under my breath in the key of doubt
as you pray to the god of washrooms, *make us clean.*
Each day's bitter ribbon and its calculus of light. I sing o *bastard of my heart*
be still. Your god is the god of mirrors, and the house a paper wasp builds
is paper. There are broken slats in every tiny thing. The pupa
and its carapace. The celery salt, the stalk. The way my birchy skin
peels off. Your hennaed hand. Your hand. How grief runs
through me like a pack of eels. Silver and colloidal,
the tides have seen us coming and turn back.
Like them, our work is breakage. To plunder *to* from *fro.* Inside us
something pliant, soiled. Bearing the dent of thumbs.

drag king manifesto

That woman is an engine, I refuse. To generate. To be chambered. To combust.

Let her who would acquire don the masculine article. The necktie and the
        wingtip and the *the*.
The leather chair, its kingdom. As wispy shadow tidies in the wake.

I too unhitch my notice. I touch what I will touch. I wear
        roulette-wheel cufflinks
and filch the jack of diamonds from the deck.

I'll show you how to razor: Take off your gown of ghosts. Untie
        your solaces, unzip your name.

Let her who would be pirate begin in piracy. The double-breasted suit.
        The clamp.
Adam's apple pendant in the throat.

Let her who would go veiled take up her wrench, her drill. Up her sleeve
        the jackal of hearts, the jack of jills.

Let her in frilled distress begin. To study the mallet, the screw.

And therefore tinker. Therefore crux. How treason wears the pants.

Let her who would go naked smith her tool.

aegean

posit a hull unbroken
in the broken book of sky

seam of air and water
whelps   the hard blue furl

the lunar sailor   pricks   her oar
unsex me now   o sun

the splayed   sea is not
female   nor the boat

the sky's diminutive   freights her
hard at the starboard rim

red right returning   drags its net
for sun-hubbed   basilisk *she*

sheets to the wind   her sailcloth   *logos   teleos*
she calypsoed   she odyseus

horizon's wire   sharps its edge
her alphabet   scatters   like a sack of wind

as under oceanic gaze   her cyclops
sex   unlids its spindled eye

whose keel   refutes
her charter   childless

codices   days   porous
the periphery   is vast

inerrant scud   the map   spools off
salt like the body's

eros   opals not
the sea

shibboleth

A florida I enter in
the name sends out its spikes.
The name is a pod
for the child.
See how the self
rattles around inside?

And such similitude
of love. I am hove up.
A rope to apprehend.
Barnacled. As instinct.
A hand to shuttle forth.

As if our increment were whole:
the pouring-out of waters
over stone,
a shelf of grasses, pressed

beneath the wave.
Or gill net, opalescent
gill. A substance to refute.
Omit the sibling fist
of wind, the hook,

the redundant gale.
Here the tongue will sorrow forth
its crisp and bloody pod.
The seed is always mute. A cut
exposes the wifely pith.

dredge

this harbor for anything   what can be salvaged

or not   salty engines   spinnaker poles and bones

no bells   no letters in bottles   but bottles   void of pills

as seaslick resins harden on the birds

my captain   what port   what anchor

you order us drinks with a twist

though after a simple gin I'm sopped as bread

a single helix of lime   lies down in my glass

and look   my obedient teeth   how they line up in their pews

await the holy spirit   of your spit   o captain

what big jibs you have   what jumble of hooks and nets

what bluefish swarm and school in you   what codfish

salt you down   deep in your holds are mudfish   krill

rendered flesh of whales   lampreys   heavy metals   things that spawn

transit

A whole air stricken. Flash and count.
A freight train splits the crossing, pushing ahead of it its cone of light.

How the rage of effort equals the rage of *I*. As cars tilt past,
a film reel's grainy frames. What's lonesome in you

heaves and jerks, a severed arm beside the right-of-way.
Or how, on a different train, the passengers sleep for hours

with their dreams of pie and sex and rusty gears. Scenery
doesn't interest them: the orange moon pressed against horizon's skin,

the silo's phallus jutting toward its sky. Soon they'll sleep past scrapyards
full of gleaming, broken cars. Two rails rush and simmer at their feet.

What tempts you is the crossing. The slaughter's easy yaw.
As if in the cant of wheat fields, some prophecy, as yet unread, abides.

mapping the moon

Now to map such privacy. Now to shoot an azimuth toward the known.

Patience, damage, history. These are consolations, subjects studied at removes.

Now to chart division. A silence we ingest. The ancient pock

of gender, its tattered beds of light.

Sea of pathos, sea of veils, sea of barren brides

We supervise such darkness, the crater's frozen ring.

The mountains are a harbinger. White to scald the eye.

Here in the zone of names, our motions fall to dust. Discarnate

female surface,
chemical, immune—

The knucklebone by which our lots are cast.

Sea of disinheritance, sea of the hungry dead

We moor in the crater's shadow, its blank veracities.

To wince in silver slipper. To lay a path unto.

2

enumeration

Go to the window. Count the birds.

How many seagulls are there? How many cries?

You must work hard. Like this. Like this.

The single musical phrase practiced over and over.

The work is intricate he said, running his fingers

over the carved green wood. Sometimes it was iron,

sometimes tin. Tin squares on the ceiling

and every one a branch, a flower, a leaf. Crystal

in the window seemed most beautiful in the sun.

The small cut circus. The dog with small gold teeth.

The light as it looked coming through the leaves

on that particular summer night, when I was eight

or nine. The light and its withering into dusk.

The circle, sometimes leaf and sometimes

stone. The single recitation, over and over:

I said *He leadeth me into pastures*

of green and gold I made

it up I said *He maketh me lie down*

beside the still, blue waters,

where all is still and still is still

the work is intricate

where He annointeth my head in oil

a single musical phrase

in the presence of mine enemies

the buzzing of the mower. The buzzing

of my father, working harder. How

many seagulls, then? How many psalms? Or
was it water, running from the hose?
I do not count the cries of gulls.
I count the birds in flight, the stones, the picnic table.
The girl who found the mussel on the beach.
The single stand of crabapple, like smoke.

wonders of the invisible world

We mowed the lawn by incandescent light
and fell into a marvelous affliction
of speaking   felt that we   were borne
up from the lawn   *that room*   of grass
the leaf   the bark   the tuberous white root
wholly by an invisible force
a great way toward the sky—
and levitated   *tip to tip*
the orchard boughs   the scent so hot of night
the breath remembering the breath
her breast not being covered
spoke much of a white spirit
could not have been   dissembled
I touched her breast   *her discourses*
the great implausible elm
our garments lost upon the air
for who can give the reason
and floating through the cherry-limbs
so touching the doctrinals
upon volition   of the human soul
the hand should then be lifted through
the foil of the night
to touch   be touched   *if witchcraft be*
as I suppose it is   the juniper that moment
alight in ghosts   or flames

summer is the season for cutting back

My father's mower roars and drones,
the edge of evening frayed beyond its use. Puffballs
haunt the graying lawn. I hear the grasses' faint, nocturnal cries.

As if it mattered. As if it could have mattered:
a small bag, filled with small things. Hidden
and discovered (*Is this yours?*) after only an hour had elapsed.

Summer, my father tells me, is the time
for pruning back. Every tree around us bears this scar.
I watch him from the cherry tree, its black and supple limbs,

the sad moss mounded thickly at the root, the ladder
of the lower branches cut, and always
my difficult climb. I could not

stop. I could not be stopped. A small girl
filled with small things: the spider on the leaf,
the bark's rough curl, the sudden sun receding from the trees.

Or say not *I* but *she*, not *he*
but *they*. She searches in the dusk while someone shouts,
then slips toward the wooded edge

as if she would lift the grass and slide beneath, then let them call
and call. There's nothing in their voices that could love
the dark mass of the elms, the gathered birds—

She hovers in the hour, resolute. The leaves
become a temple of gray light. Cherry branches touch
her thighs. The bony roots of trees

extend, but slowly, coldly. Something ancient
waits. And it is this
to which she is betrothed.

the cipher

the bright day pooled around me   water

glimpsed through leaves   *taken*

with trembling and striving   the path

growing jagged with stones   *a black dog*

passed before me   in and out of the trees

the wind died down   *I thought myself alone*

there came a woman to me   out from under the trees

dressed in blue   *blue skirt blue cap blue coat*

a strange frame in her countenance   the sunlight

played   her face   the bright leaves

darkened around her   *she took me*

by the hand   and led me under the pearmain tree

conjunction of blue shadow   *I was so bitten*

I could not lie still   a strange place   *naked*

about her breasts   and taken with strange fits

her hand grown cool upon my skin   *I smelt it sweet*

like cider   then she was gone   *I knew not where*

the lindens   quivering   a black

crow in the tree limbs   *a very great quick eye*

she looked at me   the cipher

concealed in all things   stirred

and then it blinked   and vanished

as if through a chink in the board

having been put to bed

The night I walked out of my bed, shadows threw themselves across the driveway. Voices drifted through my window. *No. Do you believe it?* No. Outside the window, fireflies were falling bright and thick. *Catch as catch can,* someone said. But I was climbing, leaf by leaf, to where the elm tree slowly netted the moon. I threw the snagged stars back into the grass, where they lay bright and thick and did not burn. Down below, I saw my father, pruning in the dark. *Catch,* I called and threw him one. It was he who found me. Walking barefoot in the grass, saying *spark* and *plume.*

after so many years

Last night I dreamed that starlings flew
past the windows, massing in the trees.
Like something from Ezekiel, you said.
I partly understood the tongues they spoke in.

This morning, lightning flickers in the hills.
Hornets fling themselves against the glass.
Something living rattles in the walls.
The book falls open to the word 'desire.'

How does the dowsing-rod know when to shake?
How does lightning know which oak to crack?
Daylight binds the fire in my limbs
to distances and so much open air.

in medias res

Before the day grows hot, she wakes to the drone
of bees. She fastens the braid of her leaving, hooks
her shadow back to the wall like a coat.

She counts the pieces of dreams: ten black birds
and a coin. Coastline where a blue house
waits with its rooms like hearts.

Now when she hears them talk
she knows how the story will end. How can she leave
this orchard, embroidered with loss?

Things do not even have names
other than those she gives them. Light threads her veins
like a needle. She knows no tense

for this. Where are the people not
her own, their rooms in order, their city lodged
in ice? The almanac has no chart, the atlas

no pale map. At night she slips out
like a cricket, follows the shape of the trees, touches
the mulberry's branches, blackened

with fruit. Always before there has been
no way out of the garden. Now she hears him saying
Thou shalt not. The path beneath the trees

cleaves as the words like snow
swirl around her. This, she thinks,
must be the beginning of time.

transparence of the seen

In the garden everything bloomed at once:

jonquil, iris, thorn. Spring was slow and adamant.

Sight inflicting itself. Was this

the fall? Was this the scripted loss?

The fragile aptitude of frames.

A blind coherence of grasses.

The unbound universe unbound, tumbling space upon space.

The frame, exposed, could not be altered.

What was to be trusted, what believed?

She said *flesh* and *tether*

to herself. Unbound blossoms

drifted through the garden, starlight

gone to fossil in its travel. So many zones

of sanctity, so many lost and fallen explications.

They sat together on the porch

noticing the scrape, scrape of the wind.

She watched the fresco of her lover's eyes,

the flint of dawn, the frugal veil of clouds.

lineage

A bird flies out of the stovepipe as the shadows of pears lengthen in the evening. The smell of mowed grass rises through the window. I pass behind the window-screen, thinking about the white cloth shaken out after supper, about the thick translucent cloth of sky. *She simply disappeared. Last seen wearing bluejeans. Brown skin, blue shirt, blue.* Knapsack. Kidnapped. Runaway. *And so much nothing in between.* Running as only she can run, the three pears in her pocket cutting a milky path through night. Inheritance of sidewalks, lineage of stars. Run, I whisper, twisted metal, three sweet pears to stars. Spirits speak you tongues, will speak you there.

discoverie of witchcraft

> For common justice demands that a witch
> should not be condemned to death unless
> she is convicted by her own confession.
> The *Malleus Maleficarum*

hot coin pressed   to her forehead
a clear and subtill voice   silver the hot
of her knowing   *whose Sunne hath dominion by day*

at twilight the cold star of Saturn   birch limbs
brittle as bone   *each in her left hand a torch*
ahead of her lost   in snow

trackless her body   arching   *teats*
in her privy parts   temple her temple
whose hidden   *that had been lately sucked*

bird of her breathless   beating   caught
to and fro in their riddles   trackless
prison   *pricked in every part*

> *Did not you come out of the snow in likeness of a stag*
> *Did not you arise from a branch and become a bird*

her throat   ablaze   in darkness   *shaved*
in her secret   gleam   the grip of air
her fastened lung   *a fear where no fear is*

eye of her scathing   *two black spots*
between her thigh and body   blank
as morning   kept   as the narrow day

> *Did not you spit in the wheat fields and thereby cause great drought*
> *Did not you spoile all orchards and greene corn*

fruit of her snarled woodlot   *that men cannot*
beget   thornapple   bloodroot   *knowing*
the power of trees and herbs

those engines brought before her
stave of her marrowed   hand   interstice
and ratchet   cusp of her shuddering   joint

> *Did not you collect the members of men and shut them up in a box*
> *Did not they move   therein   like living members*

window her hewn   the gape   her wide
our sickles crack'd and broke   edge
of the opening   vise she cannot

window the voice   her every   *being*
more tightly stretched   window the hot
I have not done these things

> *Did not you pronounce strange words at the place where two roads meet*
> *Did not the devil appear in a violet flame*

watched in her flickering   tongues of hair
the winds by conjuration   the latchless sea
her churning   flesh unlatched

her armes through branches' mesh   in thickest
shade   *jerked up   invisible fire*   lashed
within   *that cannot be contained*

>>> *Do you deny you gave birth to twins and buried them alive*
>>> *This afterwards thought some other   natural death*

the threshold ruptured   frame of no   *to loose her*
to confess   the hinge   wrenched back
at last begins   the moment   splintered mirror

>>> *Admits she made a red horse die   by means of a powder her lover*
>>> *Says she had not wanted   to do harm*

that lath   of bone   the lintel cracked
a swallow on the rafter   spake
and bade her write   the knuckle split

>>> *Says with thrie other women   she dansit a devilische danse*
>>> *Near the mill   in a meadow   filling their pot with bloud*

her tongue a latch   *to name them*
just as I   myself   my hands   my legs
unutterable   room

Admits they made from bones and limbs   an unguent   easily drunk
And trod the holy wafer underfoot

admonished to think
of her conscience   instrument
of locked

when I had said this I was left in peace

admits without compulsion   being a creature wrought
by humours much afflicted   and much abused with fits

for spirits have no flesh and bones
writ in the book of death   this
our definitive sentence   she ratifies and confirms

cannot this hunger be holie

who lifteth her hand to write
who understandeth the singing of birds

this she confesses   to be

from a rafter

Thrust toward a kind of stubble light. Slave to what is, slave

to what is seen. Blank of the lakewaves flicker,

flinted-in. How to undertake: the mown, the whittled field. Swallows

lifting mud against the sky.

Who will take up the sheaves of hay, unload

new lumber from the beds of trucks?

Basins of sudsy water spilt out on the grass.

A sluice. An acreage banqueted in rain.

A muddy ditch in which appears the pale slip of a face.

On the sill, a chain of wasps—

Who will take up the handsaw,

the splintered handle of the pruning shear?

Beguile me a list, an antiphon of hope.

Beget for me a season, a sustenance crusts.

3

grief street

Thailand, 2005

If not for the ship's hull liquoring
light, the day's bent edge, the arc
of a traitorous thought, if not for thresh

and thrash in my blood like a thousand bells, then
anise and white silk would lay us down,
then we would lick the scene

as a tomcat preens its belly, static-struck and pure
attention bent to slipknot
the way a greenbottle fly

alights on a grain of rice. How to bind up, meddle, knit
bone and potsherd to their scab of noon? How else
to quench and stutter down (icy cloud-spur,

splint of rain) the carcasses we spatchcock,
swaddle, eat? In the sunburned plaza women sell their wares:
votive papers, coffins, and red thread. Children

shout from crevices and grease from many fingers
smuts the wall. As it is written
none may know the hour. For a long time

there is only waking up: the little
heap of salt, the broken pot. Then a tinny

warble in the throat. Cooking oil tendrils up

as incense in the temple sucks its coal. How to carry. Heave
and heave. How to stitch the breath.
Where wallets and torn flip-flops clot the beach

as each day's crushed trucks wash in on the tide.
Shoeleather burns on the trash-heap
and another acrid smell

of diesel fuel and rubber, sour fruit—
sinks among the banyan trees and monks
whose saffron chant can't enter us

your body dense with suffering and lymph
as mine is, and we do not read
the script in which some solace may be writ.

The market offers up its carts of roasted fish, stalls
of lemon and lychee, splintered bowl
and tongue. Here all the steps we take are loops

threading us to traffic, *tuk-tuk*, sky—
whatever licks or steadies us, horizon's silver rail
leading us backward, sticks of joss

lit in the levening stench, in the evening haze.

khao lak paradise resort

Thailand, 2006

She scrubs the courtyard with a ragged broom
as red ants climb and bite. In the morning,
every morning, there is rain.

Something tourists look at. Something to consume.

Bottles of amber gasoline
ranged on a roadside stand.
Blue plastic funnel swinging in the wind.

How to compass a country: my glasses
smeared with sweat.
Now our grief is put away—

Green loops of jungle overtake red road.

*

Papaya trees and bo trees,
corrugated metal on the sand.
On the shoreline, mattresses,

bottles. Bookbags. Clumps of string
where the ocean, having eaten
recedes to chew its cud—

*

Later, we ride in trucks
past boats that ploughed ashore
Orange Devil and *Blue Angel*

propellers sunk deep in the clay.

Everywhere, framed faces of the dead.
As if they have yet to discover.
As if a *when* existed,

as if a *where*.

*

The sun is a finger pushing through
the plastic sheet of sky.

*

Skin of the morning breaks
her body the color of teak
she scrubs the courtyard with a ragged broom

as a shrimp farmer checking his crop
holds a jar of water
to the light.

Through the jar
there are people running.
Through the jar, a wall of black sea.

Then there was not one bird sound. Not one dog.

*

I heard the water coming, the sound of breaking glass—

     Trees and roots were stuck across a door.

       I said to myself, Patrice, you have to break your leg.

       To become one with the water, not to fight.

I took a breath of water.
I began to kick and die.

At first it was very painful in my body
then it was very beautiful
sound and light

*

Mei dei, she says, *could not*

the child swept from her arms—
A yellow gecko ripples down the wall.

*

On the razor-wire fence
their bodies sliced like soap—

*

As if to enumerate. As if to begin.
But the bag of salt I carry in my sack
cannot suffice

for her body the color of teakwood,
for the gold and sodden color
of her name.

*

When we washed up, we were naked.
I hung by my foot from a tree.

Smell of fish and sewer, salt and mud.

*

A night sky filled with birds

op op   grip grip   of frogs.
In the hall, our sandals wet with sand,
green jungle and red earth.

The one white thread that binds us all
held in the hands of the monks.

And the tree had yellow flowers.

A leaf embossed with rain
scent of onion
crushed in the soiled air.

*

Months after, on the beach,
someone asked him for a cigarette.
When he turned there was no one there

but he felt a thump on his chest.

Then he spoke in English for an hour
—this is verified—then he said
in *English*, I want to go home.

*

New houses

calamine-lotion pink
but we paint the child's room white

The ocean offers one blue palm
as if to show it's empty
then spits up a bone—

*

How to compass a country. How else
to begin. *Evil spirits bent the tree
on which the ocean rests—*

As the child framed by muddy road
waves to our passing truck
recites from her father's arms

hello bye bye

ignis fatuus

I do not believe in the one great plan.
The Maker folding the edges of the single paper crane that is a life.

Or that this morning's silky fog is more than an illusion, more than mirror.

A yogi told me once, *I don't know how to stand.* A dancer, *I can't walk across a room.*

How to tell sky from water, sky from land. Each day's identical transit
and the same derivative landscape. Colonized.

A cigarette-tip on asphalt shatters into spark.
The cinematic moment, there then gone—

The way the human silence curls around you as you drive, sleek
as the inner surface of a shell.

A little mind could live in there, the little greeny gobbet of a heart.

Imagine vast concordances of mind
inscribing, night on night, a furl of dream.

Yours and only yours.

Tempting, isn't it?

If I believed there were an atlas, I'd study these blanks of road.

If I believed there were a road, I'd pack my car with water and set out.

But how to believe in an *I*. Everything argues against it.

Like ocean crushing houses, sweeping the fleeing children from their bikes.
Their lungs fill up with water,
grains of sand
swept back under the door.

torque

on the number line of error   I am one
as if a sparrow   (wrecked   of solitude)
    reeled from its sky   a sparrow   gone clumsy

    in its wing   (wound where septic   burrow
swells)   and if there is a rooftop   buoyant   lipped with fog
    then there is also rubble   tossed out   by the sky

    the way the buildings bide their years   as crows fly out
of her throat   because the sky is its own mouth   and *I*
    a single letter   in alphabets of grief

    the *after*   in the *aftermath*   an apostolic light
whose rain is only harbinger   trash cans filled with birds
    keys left in doors   another kind of vow

4

formulary for a winter landscape

Past the wreck of the cattails, the oriole's sodden nest,
empty water opens, olive-blue. The harbor, wind-scuffed,

flattens out to the still horizon-line. The sky is a silent slate,
etched by a single gull. This is the locked

zero of the year. Only the frozen marsh-grass moves.
The days recite themselves as if by rote.

I thought I had forgotten winter's austerities:
the treatise of the low-slung sky, the air's dense argument.

The pale, allotted sunlight. I gaze from the harbor-edge
at the blank mosaic ice floes, the water's wash and clink.

The wind is irrefutable. A black dog runs the shore.
I watch as its shadow slips toward the dunes' blue shade.

Bereft, I cling to the ruin: the chime of a boat's stripped mast,
the twisted pod of the locust-tree, the heart's blank offering.

Our summer has renounced itself. Bare as an upturned palm,
I cede my love to solemn air, to the staring glass eye of cold.

crossing to chebeague: december in casco bay

For Anne Porter

Driven for once below deck, I watch
as the snow spins down, squint
at pines in the distance: the thaw
is a long way off. A little smoke leaks
from the houses. The water fills with snow.
The cabin smells of diesel fuel
and wool. These, then, are the islands
from which you launch your life:
actual fishermen glancing, thinking *stranger*.
I think of you crossing this water
before school every year,
of your father bringing back groceries
dressed in his big gray coat.
From Japan you send me paper
pale as a luna moth's wing,
stamps with warblers, a card
with a tiny deer. *All I can read
are the numbers*, you write
from Kashiwa. *I get very tired of using*

only the smallest words: 'Japan
is a good country; Japanese people
are nice.' There are goats across the street
that I stop to talk to each morning.
They eat their fill from gardens devoted
to radishes and green tea. The engine heaves
through the water. Which of these islands
is yours? We scrape past houses built
at the edge of a cliff. One road rings
the island. Your whole house smells of books.
The stairs to the attic pull down by a string.
We cut the tree in the evening, talk on your narrow bed.
I sleep near the woodstove, wake when the fire
goes cold. In the morning, sun comes slanting
into an old red chair. I dream you are curled
and reading, there where the windows
face south. *This is our ration*, I tell you, your dark
hair made more dark. *Ration of sunlight, spent*
in a sun-starved place.

vision

This morning a single crow
flies from underground. The crow
is an invisible hand, moving
inside a black glove. There's snowmelt over the orchard. Ice
on the river thins. But morning's grey, as ever, and *thaw*
is a mourning dove's cry—
blank as that seamless water,
exhaling a little mist, which, in the myth
precedes creation's breath.

When the doe appears in the orchard
she's more a vision than real. (Nefertitti, weightless in her barge
of olive wood and rose gold. A helmsman
guides them through the steaming waters. Her slim head
gazes toward the afterlife...)
But the doe is heavy, fleshed in her animal smell.
She nuzzles the ground, flicks back an ear, looks up. The ear
is a tree of blood, poised
in a sovereign light. Her skin
the transparent scale of ice
looping the river's pulse.

She must have lived all winter
on hemlock-browse and bark. Rickety
as a shed now under her winter coat
she paws at the crust in search of a missed apple

one that's lain all winter, clenched
in snow. Her feet are a quiver
of knives, her head a chiseled spear.
Every muscle's an arrow, nocked
to its bow. Now, as she lifts her head

an old intelligence
holds me in its alien regard.
Between us, the skin of species
hangs—a hide across a doorway.
Then something silent shatters in my core
the way a maple tree explodes
under the night sky's empty platter of cold.
And night limps on, no one around for miles. *Species*
is a drifted field, too deep for us to pass through.
Her gaze is a water's black expanse
swallowing white flakes.

In a year, her bones will lie in their cave of snow.
Crows will scatter her carcass after the thaw.
Today, her tracks are toothprints
on the hill's perimeter. A snow like vellum
starts to fall. It piles up
in the notch of a stripped black tree.

snowed in at the botanical garden

For Anita

Alone in the canceled afternoon,
we wander the glassed-in garden, our own
domed paradise, unearthly green. Unseen, we stroll

past the fountain, follow the narrow path, slip beneath
the topiary lion's steady gaze. We enter the maze
of jungle. The air is heavy, hot. We leave the pathway, step

through a thicket of fern. To our left, enormous dark green leaves
float at shoulder height. To our right, the dense lianas
twine their heavy fingers through the trees.

This is the kingdom of blood lily, queen's tears,
flaming sword; we push through the green past angel wing
and adder's mouth, past the black prince

fig, the blindness tree. We touch the kapok's thorny bark,
the gnarled ebony; stoop beneath a drape
of spanish moss. In the gloom, the pale moth orchids

glow with ghostly light. We hold our fingers up
to their cold, white lips. They do not breathe
from their speckled mouths. They watch us, as the dead

watch the living: insensible, remote. We peer ahead

toward the open air, press through the tangled brake; tumble,

finally, into the hot gray light. Now we stand

at the center, the apex of the dome.

Above us, palm fronds push

against the glass. Waterfalls churn at the edges,

but here, at the garden's heart,

silence—a wide emphatic bloom—fans out. We glimpse

through the thick hibiscus, the sleepy silver eye

of a pool that lies half-hidden

beneath the overgrowth. Above it, mute red trumpets flare

and close. We move through the ponderous silence, drawn

toward the garden's core: a stack

of moss-flecked granite, one low

and scraggy tree. And there, beneath the tree,

beneath the dome, a litter of yellow fruit

circles the trunk like a saffron robe

at the feet of a shivering bride. But these

are squandered riches. Pungent, overripe,
the fruits lie burst on the garden floor
their split skins lined with rows of small brown ants.

Only one is whole: a smooth, translucent egg.
You reach past the jagged line of rocks, pluck it
from the dirt. The fruit is heavy, speckled, cool as wax,

perfectly formed to fit in the palm of a hand. We hold it
to our nostrils, search the trunk for its name: *Ambarella.*
Winter-blooming fruit. Ripe, unblemished,

fallen, we cannot help but eat. We share this flesh
in the garden's failing light. It tastes
of apple and lemon, its pit

a thorny star. Outside, the frozen city
slumbers, turns. The snow
continues falling. Above us, the amber fruit

hangs suspended
past our reach. We listen
through the dark: we hear it drop.

the visions at lascaux

Bison, limned in charcoal, die across the rocks.
Reindeer float in ochre on the walls.

Overhead, soot rings the opening;
the river froze, careening into cold.

Then, as now, the moon spun through the trees.
The people watched, with sorrow in their bones

and night stretched long. The pressure of a mouth,
the thumb-smudge tracked across the flute of bone

while ice and lightning crackled on the ridge
became the cry that pared the darkness down.

They must have tracked the fire as it fell
and heard the great oak snap as something struck—

daylight found the trunk still smoldering
threads of smoke escaping from the bark

as if the god inside still fought the god
that ate its heart and left its entrails black.

That night the shaman dreamed the dream of trees
fading from the cliff between the worlds.

They lit a flame to guide the shaman's sleep
as they waited, in that low-roofed place, for spring.

natural selection

The leaves are a filter above us, the lobes infused
   with light. We wake to a shriek
      of warning, a trace of shadow
         pulsing
            in the trees.

        How long it takes
      to waken, the forest patched
    with shade: liquid
      birdcall

    falling through

  our sleep. But this is not
the garden. When we wake in our cage of limbs

       earth is already broken,
        continents
       adrift;
       the forests long extinguished. Our ancestors
        already indistinct.

    Now we wrack
      the branches, the sun
        too soon grown bright.

Chatter spreads among us—

Clips its minor circuit through the trees.

2

One of the lemurs, an albino, falls to the forest floor. Injured,
it does not survive; dies of what is perhaps
an inherited weakness.

In dreams we are always
        falling, our bodies taut

                with fear

                        as we cry in our broken
                                language through the limbs—

The mother remains behind all night. Her infant
will not rouse. The troop moves on.
At first light she rejoins them.

                (We wake in the dank
                of the body, that shelter thatched
                                with doubt.
                        Accident of sweat and matted hair.)

The gibbon, plummeting downward, utters no cry
of alarm. Calmly it reaches, grasps
a limb; swings off in its

> *original direction.*

3

We cleave to the myth of choosing: ourselves
the chosen ones. Shaped by natural
accident or intent.

Consider:

The strong
do not survive.

The oceans swell
and change. The frail
have forms more perfect
than our own.

Think
how the flexible weak
adapt:

The hydrocephalic child
will die with the sound of water in its ears.

Its skull, like a flower, opens.

The days pour down like light.

Contemplate
the ancient

mudfish, animal
too fragile for our sea.

at the river llushin

i

These waters are not a color that anyone would believe:

say, jade-green or tourmaline,

chrysoprase, frothed

with white—

For millennia the stones

spread, an alluvial plain

sculpted by the waters

as by hands—

One finds remembered shapes

the curvature of dream

or call it

lithograph

this meaning

formed in stone—

metamorph

or *emblem*

and the great, striated rock

borne through the jungle on foot

to fetch back rain—

Here the *Morpho* comes to drink

and an insect, call it gnat,

lies crushed

in the leaves

of my book—

The accident that place is

graphed against the accident of time.

ii

Ralegh writes, *Guiana*

is a countrey never sackt

Shee hath yet her Maydenhead

(one sees the dream

in his eye)   *the graves*

have not been opened for gold

nor the salt of the soyl spent

nor the Images puld down out of their temples

In the jungle, a phantom plant

entangles the bodies of trees

vine that gives off faint-

est light

by which to find your way—

Here *guava* is not guava

but a long green pod

which, when broken open, yields

white fruit.

iii

Burton, at the jungle's cusp:

The complicated entrance

has a monotonous beauty,

and all is profoundly still, a great green grave.

Below us, mangrove and black mud,

the roots upsticking like harrows—

Later, in the interior:

succession of raw mist

the land appears to be rotten

the jungle smells of death

The language, he tells us,

copious, but confused.

Language, at the river, falls away. Surfaces
peel back.

We eat the fruit,

spit out its oblong seeds.

iv

Language is a length
        of rotted rope. Ralegh's compass,
useless for navigation, scribed him in its round

        Amongst multitudes of ilands
                Every iland bordered with high trees
                        No man could see further
                than the river   no man
        could see further   than the breach

                We might have wandered a yeere in that laborinth of rivers

the jungle dense and fissured as a brain—

                The one branch crossing the other and all so faire   and large

        its surfaces   infolding   a great prehensile net—

                one so like to another   no man can tell which   to take

Under that silent membrane, snare of an ancient dream:
                the warring trees, a litter of bulbous fruit,
        a spider, palm-sized, devouring a bird,
                        then, curled against its stalk, the old reptilian gaze

still watching from beneath the foliage.

but this it chanced that entring a river
we espied three Indians   the old one we kept   fastened
but for this
we had never found our way

My language is a sack of guns, a flintlock
poised to strike. *The river*, Ralegh writes
bicause it had no name
we called the river of the Red Crosse.

v

The name that gestures toward me is a seed
red with black, a bleeding woman's
sign. The name, *milishu muyu*
In my tongue there are no words
to name the clicks of insects, the seed,
the particular stone—
Only the old, wrecked languages suffice.

Here, at the convergence of two rivers
Eduardo tells me in the conqueror's tongue:

Un hombre sin respeto
se había instalado aquí

pero el jaguar que mira

todas las cosas que pasan en esta selva

miraba, miraba, y esperaba

por días, semanas, un mes—

y cuando la esposa de ese hombre

vino aquí al río con el bebé

y cuando estaba lavando la ropa aquí in el río

el jaguar que siempre

mira, les miró, miró

y cuando él saltó

mató a los dos

la mujer y el niño también

This means, the man without respect
is punished by the jaguar. The woman and her child
are mere collateral. The water's rush
the tooth of a living mind.

vi

In the jungle, fear the moment
that Something drops its veil—

The jaguar coming toward you

as follicles of moments

close

and only a little cry

leaks out from beneath the canopy.

when the city falls across our eyes

Quito means *the beginning*
in a language older than remembered time. This is why,
perched atop the city, the Virgin

of the Apocalypse stands and waits.
Around her, the Andes, green and threadbare,
hunker upward into battered mist,

and nine volcanoes ruminate
beneath their brow of smoke. Twelve
stars are poised to fly out

of her crown. In her hands, she holds the massive
chain which, when broken, breaks
the neck of every person still alive—

women selling mangoes on dilapidated steps, boys
on skateboards, girls who walk toward school, missionary *gringas*
dressed like Indians, concentric silver

rings around their necks; even the man
who tends the maize in the plot beside the church—
and also the neck of everyone

in every other city.
She does not worry
about the aftermath

when the crowds are resurrected
and everyone moves on, leaving
the broken houses to their dusk.

Then she will inherit the empty towns
—the ones she's only looked at from afar—
and walk alone beneath the colored lights.

In the streets, the painted clown-heads
open their mouths and smile
waiting to swallow trash on the final day.

in the jungle (tangled passage)

Beneath the veil of moss and vine
I cut for you a pretext
    of translation.

         here we are enclosed by ghastly twilight
            and one sees only frigid, sour trees

My voice is a filigreed leaf
you find on the forest floor: a wing
of lace, a scaffold
    of dry veins.

Here are a god's milk teeth,
an angry rash
of stars.

As garnet sap
spills from the carnal tree.

         among all living creatures, only a Lizard was seen,
           that sometimes stuck his head
           from amidst the moss

Here, some human, now extinct
cut the image of a bird
    in stone.

there where the peacock makes her nest,

no voice is ever heard

It lies in the riverbed where it was born.

At dusk, our tears grow hard and white

copal resin, broken

from its tree.

Their fragrance is a medicine

to burn.

the campernoyle, fastened to the earth with little roots

contracts suddenly upward, whereafter

it falls off and shrinks away

The afterimage

hovers: translucent

husks of snails

the fern's recurrent

leaf-print

the milk-blue mineral

ingrafted with its nova-light, a talisman

of rain.

Words are a machete we use to slash a path

through the ancestral undergrowth.

And where shall we go now?

Into what strategy of camouflage?

notes

wonders of the invisible world (p.17)

Italicized phrases excerpted from *The Witchcraft Delusion in New England, Volume II, copyright 1970*. The title of the poem is borrowed from Cotton Mather's treatise of the same name.

the cipher (p.20)

Italicized phrases excerpted from *Witch-Hunting in Seventeenth Century New England: A Documentary History*, 1638-1692 (1991).

discoverie of witchcraft (p.28)

The Discoverie of Witchcraft, written by Reginald Scot in 1584, was the witchcraft exposé of its time. Scot argued that witches did not exist, and that supposed witchcraft was, at least in part, a result of forced confessions.

Italicized text drawn from a variety of source texts on witchcraft and witchcraft trials, including: *The Discoverie of Witchcraft*, Reginald Scot; *The Encyclopedia of Witchcraft and Demonology*, Rossell Hope Robbins; "Lithobolia, or the Stone-Throwing Devil," in *Narratives of the Witchcraft Cases*, 1648-1706, Edited by George Lincoln Burr; "The Malleus Maleficarum," in *Witchcraft in Europe* 1100-1700; "Masika's 'Book of Sorrows'" in *The Holy Book of Women's Mysteries*, Zsuzsanna Budapest; *The Witch Cult in Western Europe*, Margaret A. Murray; *Witchcraft in Europe* 1100-1700, Edited by Alan C. Kors and Edward Peters; and *Witches and Neighbors*, Robin Briggs.

grief street (p.37)

tuk-tuk: a three-wheeled motorized cart that serves as a cheap form of transportation. In Thailand these are brightly painted in red, blue, and yellow.

khao lak paradise resort (p.39)

Now our grief is put away: Thai culture allows a mourning period of 100 days, after which the soul of the departed—and the lives of the living—must move on.

Orange Devil and *Blue Angel*: Two ships that ran aground during the tsunami. The ship later known as the *Orange Devil* took many lives, while *Blue Angel* came to a stop just next to a house, killing no one. Today the two boats remain where they landed, within a few kilometers of one another.

I heard the water coming: See the accounts of Khun Noot and Patrice Fayet in *Tsunami Stories: Thailand*, Compiled by Bill O'Leary (Image Asia).

Mei dei: In Thai, "I cannot." There are hundreds of stories of people who attempted to hold onto small children during the wave, but the force of the water was too great. Many parents, able to cling to trees or other objects, watched as their children were swept out to sea.

On the razor wire fence: A fence erected by the Thai mafia, in an attempt to steal land from the people of Nam Kem village. Half of the 200 villagers perished during the tsunami; the survivors continue to fight for their homes.

For more on the 2004 tsunami, the Thai mafia, and their effects on Khao Lak, see *Wave of Destruction: One Thai Village and its Battle with the Tsunami.* by Erich Krauss (Vision Paperbacks, 2005).

For opportunites to volunteer in the reconstruction effort, as I did, go to the Tsunami Volunteer Center at tsumanivolunteer.net.

natural selection (p.61)

one of the lemurs, the mother remains: These two sections are based on a television program chronicling the social interactions of lemurs. The narrative included a segment on the development and eventual demise of a baby albino. Unfortunately, I can no longer recall the name of the program or date of the broadcast.

the gibbon: This section of the field notes is based on Andrew W. Mitchell's description of a falling siamang (a relative of the gibbon) in his book *The Enchanted Canopy* (1986).

the hydrocephalic child: Here I paraphrase Rosamond Purcell, who describes her experience of seeing the skull of a hydrocephalic child in a museum in *Special cases: natural anomalies and historical monsters* (1997).

at the river llushin (p.65)

Italicized text is taken from Sir Walter Ralegh's account of his travels in South

America, *The discoverie of the large, rich, and bewtiful Empyre of Guiana*; transcribed, annotated and introduced by Neil L. Whitehead (1997); and from *Captain Sir Richard Francis Burton: A Biography*, Edward Rice (1990).

milishu muyu: In Quichua, the name of a seed, half black and half red, associated with women's mysteries.

un hombre sin respeto: In English, Eduardo's narrative runs, roughly, as follows: "A man without respect [for the jungle] had moved himself in here. But the jaguar, who sees everything that happens in this jungle, saw him. The jaguar saw, and waited—for days, weeks, a month. And when the wife of this man came here to the river with the baby, and as she was washing clothes [right] here in the river, the jaguar, who always watches, saw them. He saw—and when he sprang, he killed them both—the woman and also the little boy."

    in the jungle (tangled passage) (p.73)

Italicized text excerpted from *The poison tree: selected writings of Rumphius on the natural history of the Indies*; Edited and translated by E.M. Beekman (1981). Rumphius, or Georg Eberhar Rumph, was a Seventeenth Century, German-born naturalist who traveled and wrote in the Dutch East Indies.

campernoyle: a toadstool.

about the lexi rudnitsky poetry prize

The Lexi Rudnitsky Poetry Prize is a collaboration between Persea Books and The Lexi Rudnitsky Poetry Project. It sponsors the annual publication of a poetry collection by an American woman poet who has yet to publish a book of poems.

Lexi Rudnitsky (1972-2005) grew up outside of Boston. She studied at Brown University and Columbia University, where she wrote poetry and cultivated a profound relationship with a lineage of women poets that extends from Muriel Rukeyser to Heather McHugh and onward. Her own poems exhibit both a playful love of language and a fierce conscience. Her writing appeared in the *Antioch Review*, *The Nation*, *The New Yorker*, *Paris Review*, *Pequod*, and the *Western Humanities Review*. In 2004, she won the Milton Kessler Memorial Prize for Poetry from *Harpur Palate*.

Lexi died suddenly in 2005, just months after the birth of her first child and the acceptance for publication of her first book of poems, *A Doorless Knocking into Night* (Mid-List Press,2006). The Lexi Rudnitsky poetry prize was founded to memorialize her and to promote the type of poet and poetry in which she so spiritedly believed.